10.90

SOUTH AFRICA

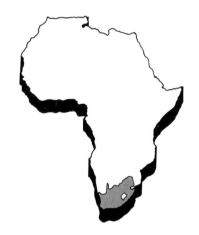

© Aladdin Books Ltd 1987

Designed and produced by
Aladdin Books Ltd
70 Old Compton Street
London W1

First published in the
United States in 1988 by
Gloucester Press
387 Park Avenue South
New York, NY 10016

ISBN 0-531-17056-X

Designer: Rob Hillier
Editor: Margaret Fagan
Researcher: Cecilia Weston-Baker

Library of Congress Catalog
Card Number: 87-80886

Printed in Belgium

The author, Michael Evans, is defense correspondent of
The Times, *London. He was formerly the diplomatic*
correspondent of the Daily Express.

The consultant, Dr Simon Baynham, is Senior Lecturer in the
Department of Defense and International Affairs, RMA Sandhurst.
He is the author of many publications on post-1945 Africa,
including Military Power and Politics in Black Africa.

Contents

SOUTH AFRICA

MICHAEL EVANS

Illustrated by
Ron Hayward Associates

Gloucester Press
New York : London : Toronto : Sydney

Introduction

To an outsider, the conflicts of South Africa are inevitably viewed through strictly "black and white" images. South Africa is a beautiful country with breathtaking landscapes, a warm climate and a wealth of natural resources. Yet it is hopelessly scarred by its political system which, by law, segregates the African majority from the white minority and discriminates against the blacks. Under the apartheid banner, the ruling white government has held total power over the country's 23 million black Africans for nearly 40 years. The blacks have no vote.

To understand the increasing anger of the blacks and the role of the white minority, you have to go back many years. The concept of apartheid, or "apartness," first appeared in the mid-17th century. Racial segregation has survived to the present day, despite pressure for reforms from both within South Africa and from the outside world.

Today the fate of the hated apartheid system and the future of the 4.8 million whites are being weighed in the balance. Reforms in recent years have removed some of the more obvious symbols of apartheid. But each reform has also heightened the frustration of the majority of the blacks. Blacks in South Africa, particularly the young, are no longer prepared to wait for the government in Pretoria to decide their future for them. They want power now.

▷ The future of South Africa depends on how the four population groups can live together. These are the whites whose ancestors go back to the Dutch colonists and British colonists; Africans who are defined as of Bantu-speaking, negroid stock; mixed race Cape coloreds whose black Khoikhoi ancestors intermarried with the white settlers; Indians who first arrived in 1860 as laborers.

▽ Johannesburg — a center of white wealth in South Africa

The history

A group of colonists from the Dutch East India Company arrived at Table Bay in the Cape on April 6, 1652. Their task was to supply food to passing ships en route from Europe to India. To protect themselves against the Khoi (the people they called the Hottentots whose ancestors had been there for thousands of years), the Dutch party built an earth fortress. This concept of isolation from the local population was to remain a key factor throughout the history of the Afrikaners, as the Dutch settlers became known. The settlers held strict, puritanical religious beliefs – they also practiced slavery.

When the British annexed the Cape in the early 1830s and subsequently abolished slavery, the Afrikaners moved up north towards Pretoria to form two republics, the Transvaal and the Orange Free State.

▽ About 6,000 Boers left their homes and with their heavily laden wagons (like the one in the photograph) and 4,000 servants, they set off from Cape Colony and headed north. This was the Great Trek and lasted from 1834 – 1854. Today these "Voortrekkers" are remembered with nostalgia, because they symbolized the whites' struggle for independence. Every year groups of Afrikaners assemble to commemorate the Boers' trek, often dressing in the costume of the time and re-enacting their ancestors' journey.

When gold and diamonds were discovered in the 19th century, the British, led by Cecil Rhodes, Prime Minister of the Cape Colony, began to expand their empire. War with the Afrikaners, or Boers (farmers) as they were also called, became inevitable. The Boer War of 1899-1902 was fierce and bloody; six thousand Afrikaners and 22,000 Britons were killed. Another 26,000 Afrikaner women and children died from disease in British "concentration" camps which had been set up by the military commander Lord Kitchener.

The Boers were defeated but in 1910, after eight years of British rule, Britain granted independence to a new Union of South Africa, formed from the British colonies and Afrikaner republics. The Boers had lost the war but now they were given control of South Africa.

△ This map shows the routes taken by the Boers during the Great Trek. The first major obstacle was the Orange River which was impossible to cross in the rainy season. Beyond the river was 500 km of hard monotonous travel. To reach Natal, their first destination, they had to cross the Drakensberg range of mountains.

▽ The Great Trek of hardship and determination

Apartheid

Under the Union, a more liberal British attitude towards the black community continued in the Cape. But in the north, the Afrikaners took the first steps that formed the foundation of what was to be called apartheid. In 1913 the Natives Land Act was passed by the ruling whites. Hundreds of thousands of Africans had to leave their homes. Special reservations, called native territories, were set aside for them. But it was not until 1948, when the National Party came to power in an election, that the policy of apartheid was written into the statute book.

The first major law was the Race Classification Act which divided everyone into four groups: white, black, colored and Indian. Under the Population Registration Act, physical appearance, language and parentage were used to define each category.

▽ Dr Hendrik Verwoerd, who was Minister of Native Affairs in 1950 and Prime Minister in 1958, was the prime architect of apartheid. He was responsible for implementing the major race laws after the National Party won power in 1948. Verwoerd, born in Amsterdam in 1901, was driven by the belief that South Africa would be a great country. During the Second World War he sided against the British and the Jews. He was assassinated in 1966.

The 23 million blacks are divided into nine tribal groups – Zulu, Xhosa, Tswana, North and South Sotho, Venda, Tsonga, Swazi and South Ndebele. Each group is allocated to separate homelands.

Over 80 per cent of the 2.8 million coloreds live in the Cape. A colored is defined under the Population Registration Act (1950) as someone "who is not a white person or a native."

Most of the 876,000 Indians live in Natal. In the eyes of the white government they are higher up the social scale than the blacks. There have been a number of violent clashes between Indians and blacks.

Today the majority of the 4.8 million whites live in the Transvaal and the Cape and speak both English and Afrikaans. In Natal where about 12 per cent of whites live, English is the main language.

△ The four groups – still upheld in today's South Africa

WHITES WAITING ROOM.

BLANKE WAGKAMER.

Other laws were passed that helped to build the pillars of the apartheid system. Particulalry important were the Mixed Marriages Act which made marriage between the races an offense; and the Group Areas Act which confines 23 million blacks to 14 per cent of the land, leaving the rest for the 4.8 million whites. Millions of blacks and some whites were moved. Under the pass laws, blacks were also forced to carry identity cards, which restricted their movement into white areas.

Signs went up throughout the country: "For the use of white persons only." Cinemas, theaters, transportation, hospitals — all were subject to the segregation laws. In some buildings, like post offices, there were partitions, with whites served on one side and blacks on the other. Above all, only the whites were allowed to vote.

▽ The enforced segregation of white and black led to many "petty" apartheid rules. Whites and "non-whites" were banned from sitting on the same park benches or on adjacent seats on public transportation. Those in charge of parks or swimming pools or other amenities were punished if they allowed races to mix.

Homelands and townships

△ Living conditions in Qwaqwa, one of the non-independent homelands

The National Party, inspired by Dr. Verwoerd, decreed that Africans who were not needed for the economy of white towns and farms had to live in separate homelands, or black national states. The 12 million Africans who were sent to the homelands, and even those remaining outside, were not part of white South Africa. They were given homelands, not South African citizenship. But in 1986 the government of President P. W. Botha was pressured to restore South African citizenship to over six million blacks living in four "independent" homeland states. It also announced that all blacks would be entitled to South African citizenship.

Townships were also built close to the industrial and commercial centers outside the homelands but not too near the expensive white homes. The best known is Soweto, situated outside Johannesburg.

▷ Ten African reserves were designated. Those living outside the areas allotted to them were moved, forcibly if necessary. Between 1960 and 1985 over 3.5 million people, mostly blacks, were ordered out of their homes. About 2,260 white families were transferred too. The plan was for these homelands to become independent, although only four have so far accepted autonomy: Transkei, Bophuthatswana, Ciskei and Venda. The reserves in reality became huge reservoirs of labor for the white areas.

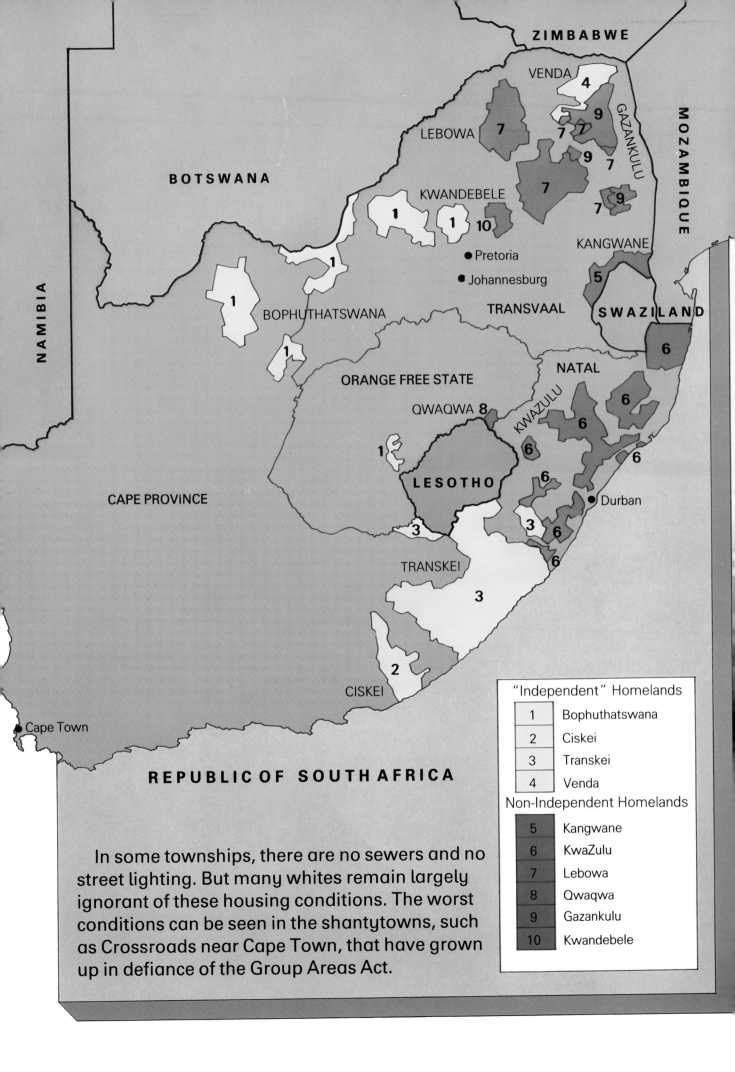

ZIMBABWE

MOZAMBIQUE

VENDA **4**

9

GAZANKULU

LEBOWA **7** **7** **7**

9 **7**

BOTSWANA

KWANDEBELE **7**

7 **9**

1 **1** **10**

KANGWANE

1 ● Pretoria

1 ● Johannesburg **5**

BOPHUTHATSWANA TRANSVAAL S W A Z I L A N D

1 **6**

NATAL

ORANGE FREE STATE

QWAQWA **8** **6**

NAMIBIA KWAZULU **6**

1 **6** **6**

LESOTHO **6**

CAPE PROVINCE **6**

3 ● Durban

3 **3** **6**

6

TRANSKEI

3

2

CISKEI

● Cape Town

REPUBLIC OF SOUTH AFRICA

In some townships, there are no sewers and no street lighting. But many whites remain largely ignorant of these housing conditions. The worst conditions can be seen in the shantytowns, such as Crossroads near Cape Town, that have grown up in defiance of the Group Areas Act.

"Independent" Homelands	
1	Bophuthatswana
2	Ciskei
3	Transkei
4	Venda

Non-Independent Homelands	
5	Kangwane
6	KwaZulu
7	Lebowa
8	Qwaqwa
9	Gazankulu
10	Kwandebele

Education

◁ Government spending on education has clearly reflected the policies of apartheid. In state schools, 10 times as much money is spent on a white pupil than on a black pupil.

▽ Schools have been a major source of unrest. It was compulsory teaching in the Afrikaans language in black schools that started the explosive riots in Soweto in 1976. The photographs show private schools for black and white. In the state schools, whites have better facilities. In 1979, pupil-teacher ratios stood at 20-1 for whites, 29-1 for coloreds, 27-1 for Asians and 48-1 for Africans.

When the National Party came to power, almost all teaching of blacks was in the hands of missionaries. But in 1953, Dr. Verwoerd introduced Bantu education. His purpose was to adapt the education system to the role the Bantu (natives) were expected to play in a white society. Dr. Verwoerd said, "If the native in South Africa today is being taught to expect that he will live his adult life under a policy of equal rights he is making a big mistake. There is no place for him in the European community above the level of certain forms of labor."

It was a dramatic statement of how the white National Party resolved to keep the black man in what it thought to be his place. In the schools, the textbooks had references to "untrustworthy and uncivilized" natives and the black pupils learned more about the culture of the white man than their own.

However, there have been considerable increases in spending on black education. In 1983 the government formally committed itself to the principle of education of equal quality for all races. Yet state schools remain segregated.

Schooling is free and compulsory for whites and Indians up to the age of 16 but is not enforced for blacks and coloreds. Only two per cent of black children complete primary and secondary education with a school-leaving certificate compared with 58 per cent of whites. Half of African and colored pupils leave school with four years' or less education. Not all schools are segregated, however. There are private schools attended by about six per cent of white children, where black parents, who can afford the fees, can also send their children.

△ In recent years, under great pressure, universities have become less segregated. There are five main universities for blacks, located in the homelands, one for coloreds near Cape Town and one for Indians near Durban. There are 10 predominantly white universities, five for Afrikaans-speakers and five for English-speakers. However, about 16 per cent of students in the English colleges are black, colored or Indian. Some of these universities have been disrupted by violence between groups of students as well as rebellion against the authorities.

Working in South Africa

△ Working in the city . . .

. . . and in the mine

South Africa is a land of great wealth and natural resources. Its three major mining industries, gold, diamonds and coal, have formed the backbone of the country's economic growth. Gold exports represent nearly half of South Africa's foreign earnings. In a part of the African continent where poverty and Third World destitution are rampant, South Africa stands out as an industrial giant.

Hundreds of thousands of migrants leave their families in neighboring African countries to work in the mines. But with about 25 per cent of South African blacks unemployed, the mass migrant labor is a major cause of dissent in the mining industry. Today the increasingly strong voice of the union leaders is demanding an end to migrant working because it helps to keep the wage levels down.

△ About 600,000 blacks are employed in the mines, many of them migrant workers, both legal and illegal from countries like Swaziland and Mozambique. Membership of trade unions for blacks was made legal in 1979 and has grown rapidly since then with the miners' union becoming better organized and more militant. South Africa's wealth is heavily dependent on the gold mines. The hi-tech stock market which trades with this wealth is almost exclusively white.

14

In 1982 the first black miners' union, the National Union of Mineworkers, was formed and two years later it called the first legal strike by black miners over a 25 per cent pay demand. It was another sign of the new mood of rebellion.

The major reform for the African workers was the scrapping of the pass laws and influx control in 1986. In the past they had to carry their identity cards at all times and anyone seeking jobs in white cities, farms or mines was strictly managed. But their wages were still far below those of the whites. Whites earn five times more than blacks in mining and four times more in manufacturing. However, unemployment once associated mainly with black workers is now beginning to affect other parts of the workforce. About 100,000 whites are out of work and many poor whites today can be seen doing menial jobs such as road sweeping and laboring. But the poorest people are the Africans in the homelands and the blacks and coloreds working on white farms, who live there in return for their labor.

Everyday life

Pressure from the black communities and from the outside world has brought reforms. A kiss in public between two people of different races was once punishable by law, but now mixed marriages are allowed. Yet there is a catch. For the mixed race couples have difficulties finding some place to live and sending their children to school because of the Group Areas Act.

The more obvious signs of segregation have gone. Many hotels, cinemas and theaters are now open to all. Some hotels have been given "international" status. But while this allows "non-white" tourists to stay in good hotels it does little for the local blacks. Not all parts of the country have stuck rigidly to the Group Areas Act, so that non-whites have been able to buy property in white districts. However this is only by violating a law which is difficult to enforce.

One of the strangest places in South Africa is Sun City, a Las Vegas style entertainment complex on the edge of the Kalahari Desert, in the homeland of Bophuthatswana, north-west of Johannesburg. Whites from the big city travel there to gamble at the casino and stay at the luxury hotels. There is no color bar because apartheid has been forbidden by the homeland president.

▷ Protas and Susan Madlala were the first mixed couple to marry legally after the South African government scrapped the law forbidding mixed marriages in 1985. However, life under apartheid continued to be so unpleasant for them that they considered leaving South Africa.

▷ The black nanny or housemaid holds a uniquely traditional role of sharing the white familiy's home life. Most white children have a nanny who often only sees her own children once a week when she gets leave from her job.

Some places such as beaches still do have "whites only" signs. Other beaches have no signs, yet blacks and coloreds have been arrested for swimming there. In one town, the all-white swimming pool was fenced off because the authorities did not want blacks to look at the whites. But there is one important sign of change, in the area of sport: today there are multi-racial teams in both soccer and track. Nevertheless these teams are still ostracized from sporting events outside South Africa due to an international ban in protest against apartheid.

Some areas of South African society never seem to change. For example, many conservative white farmers who have bought and developed their land, with the aid of cheap black labor, still firmly believe that black and white can never be equal. They cannot envisage an integrated South Africa.

The African National Congress

▽ From his cell in Pollsmoor, a prison near Cape Town, Nelson Mandela has become a symbol of the struggle for equal rights by black people. But the government which realizes that he is seen both inside and outside South Africa as a heroic figure, refuses to release him because he will not renounce violence. The government fears that a freed Mandela would lead to more violence, not peaceful negotiation.

The most important anti-apartheid organization is the African National Congress, which has been banned since 1960. Its leader, Nelson Mandela, has been in prison for over 25 years. He was convicted in 1964 of sabotage. With Mandela isolated in jail, the ANC cause is led by Oliver Tambo in exile at the organization's headquarters in Lusaka, the capital of nearby Zambia. Founded in 1912, the ANC was for years a peaceful body protesting against discrimination.

When the ANC was banned by the government, it went underground and began a violent campaign carrying out sabotage attacks. The government, in retaliation, has mounted raids on neighboring "front line" countries aimed at ANC hideouts.

△ In March 1960, 6,000 blacks gathered outside Sharpeville police station protesting the pass laws. The police opened fire. The incident was followed by police raids throughout the country and the ANC was banned.

The military wing of the ANC is called "Umkhonto we Sizwe" (Spear of the Nation). It has been responsible for sabotage attacks against power plants and military targets. But civilians, too, have been killed in bomb blasts in shopping areas and farmlands.

Violence has bred more violence. The security authorities have used an "iron fist" to suppress protest. Between September 1984 and January 1986 the security forces killed 628 blacks. But blacks also killed 327 other blacks, many of them by the "necklacing" method. Blacks accused of collaborating have had rubber tires put around their necks, which are coated in gasoline and then lighted.

The black versus black struggle is also increasing. Apart from the ANC other groups include the United Democratic Front, the Azanian People's Organization (AZAPO), the Pan Africanist Congress (PAC) and the one million member Inkatha Movement, led by the moderate Zulu leader, Chief Gatsha Mangosuthu Buthelezi.

△ Appalling housing conditions in the shanty towns which grew up in defiance of the Group Areas Act have bred anger and violence. The people of Crossroads, outside Cape Town, for example, live in abject poverty, their homes made of corrugated iron sheets and cardboard. Out of these conditions support for the ANC grows. Crossroads is a squatter town and has been bulldozed by security forces several times only to grow up again.

The role of the church

The white Dutch Reformed Church was a major influence in molding the Afrikaner character. The determination of the early colonists to remain apart from other races was in keeping with their belief that they were a Chosen People. So when the National Party came to power, the Dutch Reformed Church supported apartheid as morally justified. It even went so far as to say that blacks could go inside a white church to clean it – but not to pray.

Today, not all the leaders of the Dutch Reformed Church endorse this theology. But the churchgoers are split between those who are still opposed to multi-racial worship and the more liberal people who say that the doors should be open to worshippers of all races.

▽ A familiar sight in South Africa, the angry faces of black mourners attending a mass funeral. The dead, 20 blacks, were victims of a tragic incident outside the white town of Uitenhage, in the Eastern Cape on March 21, 1985. About 4,000 blacks had marched from the nearby township of Langa on the 25th anniversary of the Sharpeville massacre. Police, issued with 12-bore shotguns and rifles, opened fire on the crowd. Twenty died and 27 others were wounded.

▽ Desmond Tutu, the first black bishop of Johannesburg, was appointed Archbishop of Cape Town in 1986, head of the Anglican Church in South Africa. Tutu has campaigned all his life against apartheid. He was thrust into the forefront of the black/white struggle because most of the other black leaders were either in prison or in exile.

Many churchmen, black and white, have publicly attacked apartheid. Some have been arrested for their views. In 1986 the largest Dutch Reformed Church the NGK, declared that racism was a sin and the practice of apartheid an error.

The best known church leader is black Anglican Archbishop of Cape Town, Desmond Tutu, holder of the Nobel Peace Prize. He is probably the only man in South Africa who could mediate between the government, the ANC and other black organizations. He speaks out for black people, while denouncing violence. He has also called for economic sanctions against the government of Pretoria. But the South African Catholic Church fears that sanctions might cause additional suffering for blacks.

△ Hardline right-wing churchgoers who decided to break away from the established Dutch Reformed Church, (now open to all races) leave a church in Pretoria after attending a service. The new church is open to whites only.

Sanctions

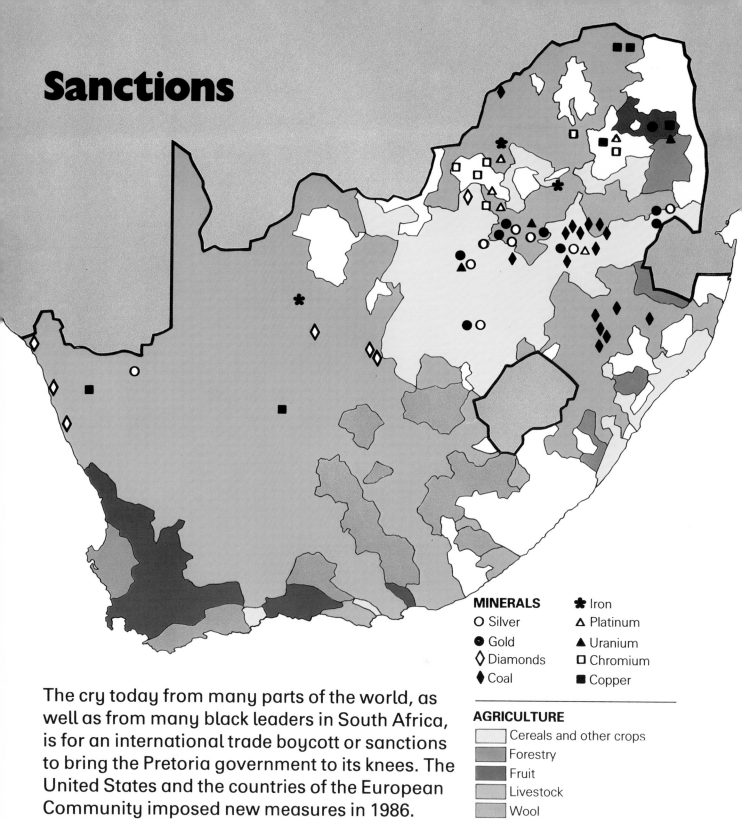

MINERALS

○ Silver	✹ Iron
● Gold	△ Platinum
◇ Diamonds	▲ Uranium
◆ Coal	□ Chromium
	■ Copper

AGRICULTURE

Cereals and other crops
Forestry
Fruit
Livestock
Wool
No data

The cry today from many parts of the world, as well as from many black leaders in South Africa, is for an international trade boycott or sanctions to bring the Pretoria government to its knees. The United States and the countries of the European Community imposed new measures in 1986. Although they have played a part in encouraging reforms, apartheid has survived.

The problem for Western countries is that they have huge investments in South Africa, particularly the United States, Britain and West Germany. South Africa's immense mineral wealth is also vital to the West and gives Pretoria a trump card in its resistance to outside pressure.

△ South Africa is self-sufficient in minerals and agricultural products, except for wheat. Raw materials – coal, steel and iron – are all exported, as well as vital minerals such as gold and diamonds.

△ South Africa's home-made jet fighter, the Cheetah, was produced in defiance of an international arms ban. South Africa's defense is among the most sophisticated in the world.

▽ The motor industry has grown rapidly since 1924 when the first Ford assembly plant was built at Port Elizabeth. In 1984, nearly 280,000 new cars were registered, the majority of them assembled in South Africa – another new area of self-sufficiency.

And yet the West, particularly those countries with a history of colonial power, feels morally responsible for helping to dismantle a system which it sees as institutionalized racism. Violent landmarks such as the Sharpeville massacre in 1960, the Soweto riots in 1976 when over 600 Africans died in clashes with the security authorities, deaths in police custody and the widespread violence in the last two years, which has led to thousands of deaths, have galvanized the West into action and isolated South Africa internationally.

Existing sanctions include a ban on official sporting links and an embargo on the export of oil and arms to South Africa. But Pretoria has responded by creating its own fuel supplies, and building a successful arms industry. Europe and the US have so far held back from imposing a total trade boycott because they fear it would harm the blacks by causing greater poverty and jeopardize their own longstanding investments.

Front line states

On the map: TANZANIA, MALAWI, ANGOLA, ZAMBIA, NAMIBIA), ZIMBABWE, MOZAMBIQUE, BOTSWANA, SOUTH AFRICA, LESOTHO, SWAZILAND

△ The black African countries that rely on the wealth and industry of South Africa have tried in vain to reduce their dependence on Pretoria. In 1980, they even formed a special organization, South African Development Co-ordination Conference (SADCC), to find ways of freeing themselves economically from South Africa. Zimbabwe imports 22 per cent of its goods, from South Africa, Zambia 16 per cent, Botswana 88 per cent and Swaziland 90 per cent. In Namibia, South Africa's virtual colony, South African forces are in conflict with SWAPO, a guerrilla organization fighting for Namibia's freedom. In 1966 the United Nations withdrew the mandate that gave Namibia (formerly South West Africa) to South Africa.

Some of the countries seeking a trade boycott by the governments of the West against South Africa are the very ones which would suffer most if sanctions were imposed. These are the nine neighboring "front line" states: Angola, Botswana, Lesotho, Malawi, Mozambique, Swaziland, Tanzania, Zambia and Zimbabwe. Despite deep political differences, South Africa is a major trading partner for all nine countries. Their economies are dependent on South Africa which also provides virtually the only reliable transportation links with the outside world.

South Africa has a complex relationship with many of these countries. While continuing to act as an economic lifeline, the government in Pretoria has punished some of the states for harboring members of the ANC, who have mounted sabotage attacks from across the borders. The South Africa Defense Force has launched hit-and-run raids against Zimbabwe, Zambia, Lesotho, Mozambique and Botswana to destroy alleged ANC strongholds.

◁ Whites, particularly near the border areas, have arsenals of weapons to defend themselves against attacks by ANC guerrillas. It is estimated that 51 per cent of white households possess firearms. Some farms have experienced many attacks. It is not an uncommon sight to see the wives of white farmers patrolling with Uzi sub-machine guns. Extremists believe that white children should also be taught how to handle arms.

Prime Minister Robert Mugabe of Zimbabwe and President Kenneth Kaunda of Zambia have led the calls for sanctions against South Africa. Yet both their countries import from South Africa. Lesotho, the tiny landlocked kingdom, buys 96 per cent of its imports from South Africa.

In 1986, South Africa closed all ports of entry in Lesotho for 12 days. There were immediate food shortages. The blockade brought the downfall of the Lesotho leader, Chief Leabua Jonathan. President Botha is thus able to demonstrate to the West that he has the power, to take counter-action against the front line states if international sanctions are imposed.

△ Mozambique is struck by devasting famine and civil war as the South African backed Mozambique National Resistance (MNR) fights government forces. Refugees from Mozambique arrive in South Africa hoping to escape the fighting, but are not allowed to stay.

Reforms and reactions

The National Party and the government of President P.W. Botha have reached a critical phase. Botha is attacked as the stubborn leader of a racist administration, who refuses to give the black majority the right to decide their own future. He has said many times that he would never allow a system of one man one vote.

In 1984 Botha set up parliaments for representatives of the colored community (2.8 million) and the Indian (876,000), but not for blacks. His step-by-step reforms have only increased the frustration of those blacks who want apartheid white rule to be overthrown – by violent revolution if necessary.

Pass Laws
The Pass Laws were finally removed in April 1986. The pass system had prohibited blacks from staying for more than 72 hours in a white area, unless they had a permit stamped on their pass book. Offenders were arrested, fined or jailed. (In 1985 nearly 133,000 blacks were arrested). But racial segregation of residential areas has continued.

▽ Eugene Terre Blanche, a former policeman, sees himself as the savior of the Boer nation. He accuses President Botha of being a weak-kneed liberal making concessions to the blacks.

◁ President Botha is pledged to "gradual" reform of apartheid. He believes that Western governments who demand an immediate end to the system should mind their own business.

The dilemma for Botha is that the rise in militancy among the blacks has been matched by growing extremism among whites on the ultra-right who follow the banner of political figures like Eugene Terre Blanche, member of a white supremacist group. They are against any reforms for blacks and they favor total segregation. Meanwhile, the West is demanding the release of Nelson Mandela and other political prisoners and dialogue with the black leaders, particularly the ANC. But Botha claims this would lead to a civil war between rival black organizations and a right-wing backlash.

▽ Helen Suzman has been a MP for 33 years and campaigned for civil rights all her life. She concedes that Botha has brought about some reforms but not enough to stop black/white tension.

▷ Winnie Mandela, wife of the jailed ANC leader, has herself been arrested and detained many times. With her husband in prison, she has taken up the fight to "free my people."

The future

The turmoil inside South Africa is growing and the country has been in a state of emergency since June 1986. Not only is unemployment and industrial unrest growing but, more significantly for the government, foreign companies and investors are leaving. Over 70 American companies, including well known names like General Motors and Kodak, have withdrawn from South Africa in the last 12 months, because of the fall in the value of their assets caused mainly by the collapse of the Rand.

There have been some signs of a changing mood in South Africa, not in the government, but among influential white businessmen. Key industrial figures, like Gavin Relly, chairman of the vast Anglo American Corporation, have held talks with the ANC in exile. This is because they recognize that the only way forward is with the white minority either losing or at least sharing power with the black majority.

◁ The press in South Africa is heavily censored. The editor of this newspaper holds up the front page which says that their lawyers have advised them not to say anything critical about the current state of emergency.

WHITE VOTES: 2,056,630
BLACK VOTES: 0

But the national elections held exclusively for white voters in May 1987 put a damper on hopes for a new era of reform. Botha's party was returned with an increased majority. So the prospects for black/white negotiations and for the repeal of major apartheid laws have receded. Yet despite the forebodings, there is still a widespread feeling both in South Africa and outside that apartheid, one day, will go.

△ The overwhelming victory for President Botha's National Party in the 1987 elections indicated that most whites either support the modified apartheid of the government or the orthodox apartheid offered by the extreme right-wingers. For the blacks the election was disastrous.

Hard facts

South Africa has an annual population growth rate of 2.7%. More than half the population are under 20. An annual economic growth of 6% is needed to create employment for more than 300,000 new job seekers. But in the last few years, because of cutbacks in the flow of foreign capital, it has only averaged 1.1%. The position of South Africa's currency, the Rand (R), has weakened. In the case of land distribution little has changed since the Group Areas Act was introduced designating 14% of the land to the blacks. The Population Registration Act also remains dividing the population into four. The charts below show how the country's wealth and resources are divided among these four groups.

CHRONOLOGY

1948 National Party comes to power

1949 The Prohibition of Mixed Marriages Act

1950 Population Registration Act, enforcing the classification of people as white (4.8 million), colored (2.8m), Indian (876,000) or black (23 million).

The Group Areas Act, which designated where blacks had to live.

1953 The Reservation of Separate Amenities Act, providing for separate buildings and services for black and white.

The Bantu Education Act, offering low expectations for black school children.

1958 Dr. Hendrik Verwoerd, Minister of Native Affairs and architect of apartheid, succeeds to premiership.

1960 The Sharpeville massacre, 69 Africans killed.

1962 Nelson Mandela arrested and sentenced to five years in prison for leaving the country illegally and organizing strikes. Later tried a second time, when explosives found on ANC's premises and sentenced to life imprisonment.

1966 Dr. Verwoerd stabbed to death by a white man and Johannes Vorster becomes Prime Minister.

1976 Soweto riots, 600 Africans killed.

1977 Murder of Steve Biko, leader of Black Consciousness Movement.

1978 P. W. Botha becomes Prime Minister after Vorster resigns following a public funds scandal.

1986 State of emergency.

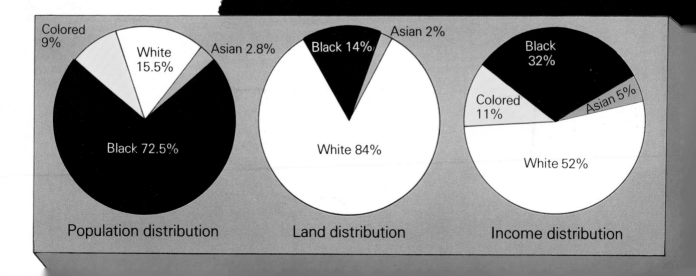

Population distribution — Colored 9%, White 15.5%, Asian 2.8%, Black 72.5%

Land distribution — Black 14%, Asian 2%, White 84%

Income distribution — Black 32%, Asian 5%, Colored 11%, White 52%

The homelands

Transkei was the first homeland to obtain independence, in 1976, followed by Bophuthatswana in 1977, Venda in 1979 and Ciskei in 1981. Another major homeland, KwaZulu, under the leadership of Chief Buthelezi, has always refused independence. The Zulu chief says the homelands are dumping grounds for blacks. About six million blacks live in the independent "national states." But Pretoria is still really in charge. The government controls the finance in the form of direct grants. The states are mostly split up which makes administration difficult. Bophuthatswana is divided into seven different areas. Transkei, the most advanced state, has its own flag, national anthem and police force. Xhosa, spoken by its four million citizens, is the official language. The independent homelands have their own parliaments with representatives elected by the black population. However these parliaments have no real power. Residents of non-independent homelands have assemblies. Residents in both independent and non-independent homelands have citizenship but no right to vote in South Africa. The homelands are not recognized outside South Africa and are home to half South Africa's blacks.

Military spending

The amount of money the South African government spends on arms and security has been rising rapidly. Spending was R44 million, 1% of South Africa's national income (GNP) in 1960, an estimated R5.1 billion, or 5% of GNP in 1986. The 1987 budget allocated R 6.7 billion for defense, a 30% rise. Made up of four services (army, navy, air force and medical), the South African Defense Force (SADF) has a standing strength of some 100,000 personnel, a fifth of whom are blacks. White conscripted national servicemen provide two-thirds of the SADF.

South African Police

Thousands of troops are deployed in the black townships in support of police operations. With a budget for 1987 of R1.6 billion (a massive 40% increase over the 1986 figure) the paramilitary South African Police (SAP) has a full-time complement of 55,000 and another 35,000 part-timers. The service – which also includes the Security Branch and Special Task Forces similar to the British SAS – is equally divided between black and white.

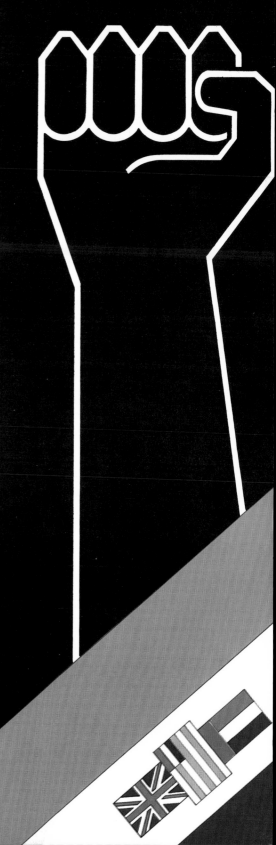

▽ A fist symbolizing black opposition, against the colors of the South African flag

Index

Photographic Credits:

Cover and pages 13, 20, 21 (left), 25, 26 (left), 27 (left) and back cover: Rex Features; pages 4-5, 12 (inset), 17, 18 and 23 (bottom): Frank Spooner Agency; page 4-5 (inset): Stern; pages 6 and 14 (left): John Hillelson Agency; pages 7, 8, 9, 18, 24, 26 (right) and 27 (right): Popperfoto; pages 10, 12 and 14 (right): Hutchison Library; page 15: Topham Picture Library; page 16-17: Associated Press; page 19: Magnum; page 21: Reuters; page 23: Mike Gething/Defense; page 28: Photosource; page 29: The Independent Newspaper.